Old Seeds
of a
New Tree

Dear Priya & Bhavani,
Best wishes,
[signature]
Oct 19/2017

Old Seeds of a New Tree

A book of Hindi-English poems

SANDEEP KISHORE

RUPA

Published by
Rupa Publications India Pvt. Ltd 2017
7/16, Ansari Road, Daryaganj
New Delhi 110002

Sales Centres:

Allahabad Bengaluru Chennai
Hyderabad Jaipur Kathmandu
Kolkata Mumbai

Copyright © Sandeep Kishore 2017
Inside illustrations by Sourav Mukherjee

ISBN: 978-81-291-4857-5

First impression 2017

10 9 8 7 6 5 4 3 2 1

The moral right of the author has been asserted.

Printed at Replika Press Pvt. Ltd, India.

This book is dedicated to

Ma,
Asha Singh
and
Papa,
Dr. Harendra Kishore Singh

for their unflinching love, affection and trust

Contents

Foreword

Old Seeds of a New Tree is a rich collection of poetry by Sandeep Kishore filled with everyday moments, plucked from a wide palate of memories. Sandeep weaves stillness and reflection intricately into his poems. He revisits conventional thinking, presenting us with a familiar, yet different perspective. The poems evoke Nature, life's rhythms and sounds, and are narrated with emotion and flair. A loose pearl falling to the ground, rolling away into silence. A door on a faraway country house, its latch clicking softly. These and several more are the fragments of life that Sandeep picks up and dusts off for them to shine.

I've witnessed Sandeep write with a unique blend of heart and mind. His poems are soulful and yet contemporary. They resonate in ample measure with our experiences and reminiscences

Harsh Goenka
Chairman, RPG Enterprises

Prologue

The affection and support from readers all over the world for my first book, *Your Shadow Wants to Walk Alone*, is immense even two years after its publication. I get many messages that poems from that book connect with you and how you see them walking as your own shadow.

There's nothing better for an author than connecting with readers in their own individual way. Many of you have also written that you started reading and conversing in Hindi again after reading the book! Thank you for your love and affection.

I am truly touched by many enthusiasts who converted some poems into songs, giving them magical, musical wings. I admit that while writing I never imagined listening to my own poems as lyrical and musical as you've made them to be. Interpreting my poems in the way they touch you is an honour. Thank you very much.

I was especially proud to see a handwritten poster with the poem *Kal Ka Suraj* designed by a group of young, bright kids at Udaan community center in Pune, India hanging in their classroom. It was heartfelt to hear their own stories and how they connected with the poem. They are the *Kal Ka*

Suraj for our society and community. Yes, children are the future for all of us. Thank you, kids. You make me smile and dream of a better tomorrow.

Each of you inspire me every day. You keep me going and urge the creative side of me to do more. So here I am again, with my second book of Hindi-English poems, *Old Seeds of a New Tree*.

Poems are like mirrors; they reflect thoughts when you read them. When you close your eyes, they speak to you. They also connect with you in your own frame and then draw you out to think beyond.

I hope the poems in *Old Seeds of a New Tree* will draw you out from the normal day to day world to a different realm. They will talk to your heart and also challenge your mind to seek higher, different altitudes.

Conflicts between heart and mind have probably existed ever since the beginning of human civilization. Whether in love or in pain, to seek or to give, to understand or to imbibe, to teach or to learn, I do hope these poems will connect with you in your own way.

Old Seeds of a New Tree has some of the most intense poems that I have written so far. I do hope you like them. I have also written several poems in this book that are on contemporary themes, each with a different take.

As with my first book, this is also a bilingual book of Hindi-English poems. Originally written in Hindi, I have self-translated them into English. Poems, much like feelings, love, dreams, joy, aspirations and hope, are universal. They need to be shared with all. I have tried to keep the core ethos of the poems similar to the original ones in Hindi, though they may not be literal in translation.

I do look forward to hearing from you! I hope you like these poems as much as I have enjoyed writing them for you. Love to you all.

1. अभी उड़ना तो बाकी है

गिर कर
ज़मीन पर
घायल से
हर ख़्वाब
टूटे लगते हैं

हर दिन
लहू से
सींचा है
रातों को
भी
तप कर
महसूस किया
बरसों तक

दौड़ा कम,
गिरा ज्यादा
हूँ
उन
पथरीली
आड़ी टेढ़ी
सड़कों पर

निशाँ
जख़्मों के
जिस्मों पर
कम,

दिलों पर
ज्यादा
होते हैं

खुदा तो
साथ है
हरदम,
दिल से
दिमाग़ की
दूरी में
हम खुद ही
भूल जाते हैं

पथ तो
ज़मीन पर
बनते हैं,
सर उठा
कर
देख ज़रा
आसमान
तो सारा
ख़ाली है

उठो
फिर से
क्योंकि
अभी
उड़ना
तो बाक़ी है

I. *I still have to fly*

When I am
down
and bruised,
when
every dream
appears
splintered,
I still have to fly

For years
I have toiled
hard,
I have felt
the burn
even
at night,
I still have to fly

I have fallen
more
than
I have run
on those
crazy and
crooked
streets,
I still have to fly

Bruises
are more
visible
on
the heart
than
on
the body,
I still have to fly

Blessings
are always
there,
I
often
forget about
them
between
the heart
and
the mind,
I still have to fly

Paths are
carved
for
the ground,
look up
the
beautiful sky

is
limitless,
I still have to fly

Get up
and
rise again,
I still have to fly

2. घर के कमरे

मैं जब भी घर जाता हूँ
हर कमरे में ज़रूर हो आता हूँ,
हवा सर्द हो या गर्म
साँसों को पता है
वो क्या कह रहीं हैं

न जाने कितने दिन,
कितनी रातें
हमने इस टेबल पर गुज़ारी हैं,
उन सारे कलम और पेन्सिल की
कभी हल्की, कभी ज़ोरों की
थपथपाहट सुनी है,
मोहब्बत के नग़में
इस पर लिखे हैं,
कैलकुलस के लम्बे सवालों को
हल भी किया है

आज भी वो टेबल
चुपचाप उस कोने मे,
बिना आवाज़ किये
हर बार मेरे आने का
इन्तज़ार करता है

दीवारों पर लगी तस्वीरें
कितने क़िस्सों की रहगुज़र हैं ये
कितना कुछ देखा और सुना है,
मैं हर रोज़

इनसे बातें किया करता था
सारे सपनों की
साझीदार भी रही हैं,
बिना कहे भी
हर बार इनको
हर बात पता थी,
मेरी आवाज़ को ये
आज भी
हर दिन की तरह
ढूँढ रही हैं

इतने सालों मे
कितने मकान बदले
कितने शहरों को
अपनाया
कितनों को
छोड़ा,
हर मकान घर तो नहीं बना
घर के कमरे कुछ ख़ास होते हैं
वो हर रोज़
ढूँढतें हैं आपको

2. Rooms of the home

Whenever
I go back home
I visit
every room,
whether its air
is
hot or cold
I breathe
and
hear its stories

On this table
I have forgotten
how many
countless
days and nights
I have
worked,
it bore
sometimes light
and
sometimes hard
taps
from all those
pens and pencils

On this table
I have written
poems of love,
and
I have also
solved
difficult and long
calculus equations
Even today
quietly
this table
in the
corner of the
room
waits for me

These pictures
hanging
on the wall
have seen
it all,
they have been
with me
a long time,
I used to talk
to them
every day,
they share
my dreams

they know
everything
when I say
nothing
Even today
as
every day
they look
for my voice

Over the years
I have moved
a lot,
I have changed
so many
houses
not every house
has become
my home
Rooms of the home
are special,
they look for you
always

3. मज़ार

जो ढूँढता रहा
तमाम ज़िन्दगी,
पता ही न था
मिलेगी वो
अपनी मज़ार पर

तेरी आँखों में
तो
हर दम देखी
मुहब्बत,
दिल का क़रार
तो
आज दिखा

आज
कुछ गुमसुम
लग रही हो तुम,
दर्द
शायद
चेहरे को
दिल की
रोशनी दे रहा है,
समय
ख़त्म
हो गया था
अगर पता होता
तो

कुछ मोहलत
और माँग
लेता

तुझे पता
तो
है,
कि मुझे
तेरी
आँखो के
ये आँसू
अच्छे नहीं लगते,
अब
फिर से कहूँ
ये
शायद मुमकिन नहीं,
हाँ
खुदा से
ज़रूर
माँग लूँगा
तेरे ये आँसू,
तेरी खुशी
के लिये
इतना तो
कर ही सकता हूँ

अचानक
याद आया,
कभी कह
ही नहीं

पाया
कि
मेरी
सारी
ज़िन्दगी
सिर्फ तुम्हारी
खुशी में
गुज़र गयी,
कहना
ज़रूरी था
ये
अब महसूस हो रहा है

अगली बार
जब आना
वो मुस्कान
साथ ज़रूर लाना,
जिस पर हम
पहली बार मिले थे
और
वो ज़ोर की
हँसी भी
जो
कभी
हमारी
ज़िन्दगी थी

हाँ,
मैं
अब भी

तुम्हारी
उसी
हँसी का
इंतज़ार
करता हूँ
हर दिन

3. Tomb

What I was
looking for my
whole life,
I didn't know
I would find
at my own
tomb

I have
always found
love
in your eyes,
feelings of
your heart,
I could only
see
today

You are
looking
a little sad,
the pain in
your heart
is
showing upon
your
face

My time
was over,
if
I knew
I would have
borrowed
some more
moments
to be
with you

You know
I don't like
the tears
in your eyes,
I wish
I could
say this
again and again,
though
I can
certainly ask
the Lord
to give
your tears
to me

I now
remember,
I should have

told you
earlier
I always wanted
you
to be happy
I didn't realize
it was so important
to say,
I always thought
you knew

The next time
you come
to see me
do smile
your smile,
the one
from
the first time
when we had met,
and also
laugh the laughter
which
used to be
our life once

Yes,
even now
I wait

for your
smile and laughter
every day

4. चलो फिर से करें शुरू

पहले
जब
फ़ोन नहीं था,
चिट्ठीयों का
इंतज़ार
रहता था हफ़्तों

लिफ़ाफ़ों को छूना,
और
धड़कनें
जैसे
पहले से
ही तैयार हो

लम्बे ख़तों को
कई बार
पढ़ना,
शुरू में
बहुत जल्द
फिर
धीरे-धीरे
और
आख़िर में,
उस तकिये को
पकड़ती
ख़त की खुशबू

फिर
फ़ोन आया,
और
आवाज़ का
जादू
लगा
जैसे छू
लिया करते
थे तुम्हें

ख़त छोटे हो गये,
बातें लम्बी

इंतज़ार करने का
तरीका बदल गया

वो फ़ोन-बूथ,
इतवार शाम
सात बजे
ओह, ये घड़ी
सात बजने में
कितना
वक़्त लगाती है,
हर एक मिनट
फ़ोन का
डायल-टोन चेक करना
और
फिर वो घंटी,
दिल के
हर तार

जैसे
झूम जाते थे

कितने
दिन हो गये,
चिट्ठियाँ
तो
कब की
छूट गयीं थीं,
आवाज़ भी
अब
कम सुनायी
देती है

फ़ोन
अब
स्मार्ट हो गया है,
खुद
बोल भी देता है
और
लिख भी

लेकिन
तुम्हारी
चिट्ठियों की
खुशबू
और
आवाज़ का
जादू
कहाँ से
लायेगा

चलो
फिर से
करे शुरू
लिखना
और
बोलना

4. Let's start again

When there was
no phone,
I would
wait
for weeks
for your
letters
to arrive

A touch
of your envelope,
and
my heartbeat
would race up

Letters
were long,
my first read
was always
excitedly rushed,
then
I would
read again
slowly
and
finally
I would read it

on the bed
to feel
the words

Then
came the phone,
and
with the magic of
your voice
I could almost
feel you

The letters
became shorter,
and
our talks
got longer

How we waited
also
changed

That phone booth
at seven
on Sunday evenings,
I would check
the dial tone
of the phone
again and again,
then

I would hear
the ring
and
my heart
would
race up with joy

Letters
already
stopped
a while ago,
now
the phone calls
have slowed
as well

Phones
have become
smart now,
they can
talk and write
on their own

But how will
they get
the fragrance
of your letter,
and
the magic
of your voice

Let's start again,
to write
and
to speak

5. दरवाज़े

पहले
सिर्फ़ शहरों के
दरवाज़े होते थे,
घरों के नहीं

धीरे-धीरे
घरों ने भी
दरवाज़े
बना लिये,
और
अब तो
दिलो-दिमाग़ तक
पहुँच
गये हैं ये दरवाज़े

चलो
फिर से
उन अतीत
पुराने शहरों
की ओर,
और
हटा डाले
इन दरवाज़ों को,
एक बार फिर

5. Doors

Long ago
only cities
had
doors

Slowly
houses
also
built them

Now
these doors
have
clamped
hearts
and minds

Let's
go back
in time,
and remove
these doors
once again

6. मोहब्बत

पाँच घन्टों
की लम्बी
और
कॉम्पलेक्स
सर्जरी

न जाने
कितने टाँके

बेहोशी से
पूरी तरह
आँखें भी नहीं
खुल रही

अपने दर्द को
किस आसानी
से छुपा रही हो

कुछ खाया की नहीं,
कहीं जगह मिली बैठने को,
कब से इस तरह खड़े हो,
अपना तो धयान भी नहीं रखते

हाँ,
यही
मोहब्बत है

6. *Love*

Five hours
of long
complex
surgery,
Lord only
knows
how many
stitches

When you
came out,
you could
hardly
even open
your eyes

How easily
you tried
to hide
your pain,
and
asked me

Did you eat,
did you find
a place
to sit,

for how long
have you been
standing
and
waiting,
You must
take care
of
yourself

Yes,
this is
love

7. कुछ बिखरे कण हैं मोती के

चुन-चुन कर
धीरे-धीरे
बहुत दिनों से
पलकों पर
बुन कर रखा है
ख़्वाबों को,
कुछ बिखरे कण हैं मोती के

वो प्यासा मन
भी कैसा है
सुनने की आदत
कम ही है
कहता ही
रहता है हरदम,
दर्द भरें हो
सीने में
दिल की
बातें
अब
ज्यादा है,
कुछ बिखरे कण हैं मोती के

अक्सर
जो ढूँढा
बाहर,
पाया है
अपने

ही अन्दर,
न जाने
फिर
भी क्यों
हर बार
चले
कहीं और,
कुछ बिखरे कण हैं मोती के

जीवन भर
सीखा
उत्तर देना,
प्रश्नों के परे
भी जीवन है
सही गलत
के आगे
एक और
नया दर्पण भी है,
कुछ बिखरे कण हैं मोती के
कुछ बिखरे कण हैं मोती के

7. A few scattered pearls

Over
a long period
of time
I have collected slowly
several dreams,
A few scattered pearls

What's with
the craving mind,
when the heart
is full of pain
it wants to
talk more
and
lay it all out,
A few scattered pearls

Whenever
I am adrift,
I have always
found
the directions
within me,
why then
do I
wander around,

A few scattered pearls

We
have learnt
to provide
answers
our entire life,
but
there is a life
beyond
the questions,
there is
a new mirror
beyond
the right and wrong

A few scattered pearls
A few scattered pearls

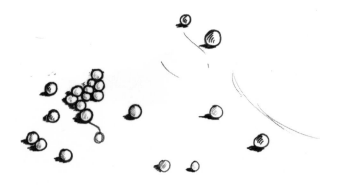

8. पहाड़ी नदी के पत्थर

पहाड़ी नदी के पत्थरों में
कुछ और ही बात है,
अल्हड़ मौजों के साथ
खेलतें हैं वो हर पल

सीख लिया है
मझदारों के साथ रहना,
तेज रफ्तार के बीच
कभी इस पलट, कभी उस

नदियों को रूख तो देना है
खूबसूरत उछाल भी,
दीवानों का हाल यही है
सीमाओं में कब रहना है

पानी का अपनापन ले कर
रूप निखर कर आया है,
मस्ती है रग-रग में देखो
बहुत दूर तक चलना है

तटों की शोभा है इनसे
धाराओं की शान भी हैं,
पहाड़ों के ये पत्थर सारे
इन नदियों की जान भी हैं

सुबह शाम जब मिलता हूँ
कुछ अपना सा लगता है,
दिल से उछलती आवाज़ें,
ये पत्थर बातें करते हैं

8. Stones from the hilly rivers

There is something
different
in the
stones from the hilly rivers,
they play with
the waves
as their own

They have learnt
to be
midstream
with the
waves,
they turn
and wobble
These stones
give shape
to the rivers,
their rise
and rippling,
much like
passionate people
always
full of
energy and ambition

Water
from the river
makes them pure,
gives them
their character,
these stones
have
fun-filled lives
they go
far
with the flow

Banks of the river
glow with them,
they are
the pride of
the waves,
stones from the hilly rivers
are also their
lives

Every
morning
and evening
when I see them
I find them
as my own,
voice bubbling
from their heart,
These stones
do talk

9. चुपचाप

चुपचाप,
कितनी बातें
हो गयी

तुमने कहा तो
कुछ भी नहीं,
लगा जैसे
बस
सब
जान गये हम

चुपचाप,
हाथ पकड़
गीली
रेतों पर
भींगे
पैरों से,
लम्बे
समय तक
काफी दूर
चलना

चुपचाप,
तुम्हारा
मुझे
करीब खींचना,
और

कभी
तेज आती
लहरों को
देखना
कभी
मयम
सी
ओझल होती
किरणों को

चुपचाप,
अपने सर
को
मेरे गोद
में
रख कर,
यूँ ही
कई घंटे
तुम्हारा
उन
सितारों से
खेलना,
और
मेरा
तुम्हारे
इन
घने बालों
से

चुपचाप,
कितनी बातें
हो गयीं

तुमने कहा तो
कुछ भी नहीं,
लगा जैसे
बस
सब
जान गये हम

9. Silently

Silently,
we talked a lot

You didn't say anything,
I knew it all

Silently,
you held my hands
and
we walked
for a long time,
along the ocean
with wet feet

Silently,
you pulled me
towards yourself
and
we watched
sometimes
the fast-moving
waves,
and
sometimes
the sun rays
falling asleep

Silently,
you
laid your head
in my lap
and
for hours
played with
the million stars
up above,
as
I played with
your hair

Silently,
we talked a lot

You didn't say anything,
yet I knew it all

10. गूगल

ध्यान से
स्कूल में
मन
लगा कर
शिक्षकों की
सारी बातें
सुनना
और
समझना

होमवर्क
करते समय
भैया
दीदी
और
दोस्तों से
पूछना

इम्तिहान की तैयारी में
लाईब्रेरी से
कई किताबों
को रेफ़र कर
सारे सवालों के
जवाब तैयार करना

अब
सिर्फ़ गूगल,

दुनिया जैसे
एक मुट्ठी में
आ गयी है

फ़ोन पर
माँ से
हर बार
पूछना,
हल्दी पहले
या धानिया
मटर-पनीर
बनाने के मज़े
के साथ
थोड़ी
गप-शप भी

छूट गयी
वो सारी बातें,
गूगल
के आने से

वो
पीपल का पेड़,
सड़क किनारे मंदिर,
लाल गेट वाला घर,
बूढ़े बाबा की
साईकिल की दुकान,
कितने सालों तक
आने-जाने वालों को
दिशा दे रहा था,

जब
गूगल
नहीं था

कहाँ जाना है,
क्या खाना है,
किससे मिलना है,
कौन सी दवाई
कब लेनी है,
वहाँ का मौसम
कैसा है,
आज
यहाँ बारिश
कब रूकेगी,
फ़्लाइट
समय पर
है
या नहीं,
सब
पता है
गूगल
को

उस मुस्कान
को
कहाँ
ढूँढूँ,
वो बातें
जो
खो गयी,

वो समय
जो
गुज़र गया,
वो कल
जो
आने वाला है,

खोज
रहें
हैं हम,
और
सर्च
कर
रहा है
गूगल

10. Google

Paying close attention
to your teachers
at school
to understand
completely

Asking
brothers, sisters
and friends
for help
when stuck doing
homework

Checking several books
at the library
to find answers
to questions
to prepare
for exams

Now,
simply
Google

It seems like
the entire world
has come into

your palm

Calls to mother
asking
turmeric first or coriander
to prepare
Matar-paneer
and also
catching up a little
while
asking how to cook,
all those calls have
disappeared
with
Google

That peepal tree,
temple at the
corner of the road,
the house
with the red gate,
old uncle's
cycle shop
For so many years
they served
as anchors
for direction,
when there was no
Google

Where to go,
what to eat,
who to meet,
what time to take
the medicine,
how is the weather there,
when will the rain stop here,
is the flight on time,
Google
knows it all

Where to look
for
those smiles,
those talks
that are lost,
the time that's
over,
the
tomorrow
that's about to
come

I am
looking for,
and
Google is
searching

11. शहर

इस शहर की
कुछ ख़ास
पहचान है

कुछ तो है
इन हवाओं में,
इन गलियों में

कितने साल
हो गये,
शायद,
दो पीढ़ियाँ
निकल गयी

अब भी
मैं जब
यहाँ आता हूँ,
अनजाने लोग
इस कदर
गले मिलते हैं,
जैसे
मैं
कहीं गया
ही न था

II. *City*

This city
has a
unique
identity

Its alleys
and air
have
something special

How many years
have gone by,
perhaps,
two generations

Even now
whenever
I come here,
unknown people
welcome me
as though,
I had never
left

12. कनेक्ट

काफी दिनों के बाद
आज फिर
खुद से
मुलाक़ात हुई

कनेक्टेड दुनियाँ ने
इतना जकड़ कर
रखा है,
कि खुद को
ढूँढने का
समय
ढूँढना पड़ता है

आज सारे
मोबाईल फ़ोनों को
छोड़ आया हूँ,
चलो देखूँ
तन्हायी
याद भी है
या नहीं

असली रिश्तों को
जोड़ने के लिये
वरचुअल दुनिया को
डिस-कनेक्ट करना
पड़ता है

मुहब्बत
अजीब है,
अगर दूर हो
तो दर्द है
क़रीब हो
तो अहसास है,
फ़ेसटाइम
की दबी
मुस्कूराहट में
वो बात कहाँ
जो तुम्हारी
खिलखिलाती हँसी
को साथ-साथ
जीने में है

लगा जैसे
कुछ
छूट रहा था,
वो कही
और अनकही
कुछ मीठी
और थोड़ी खट्टी
बातें,
जो हमारी पहचान थी
और रोज़ की
आदत भी,
वाट्सऐप
और फ़ेसबुक ने
जैसे अपने दायरे में
पकड़ रखी है

आज
छोड़ आया था
वो
कनेक्टेड वर्ल्ड

खुद को
ढूँढने में,
खुद की
खुद से
मुलाक़ात
ज़रूरी है,
वो अहसास
ज़रूरी है,
अहसास
ज़रूरी है

12. Connect

I met
with
myself
again,
after
a long time

The connected world
has gripped me
so tight
that I
have to
find time
to meet
myself

Today
I had left
all
my mobile phones,
let's see
if
I remember
solitude

To connect
and find
a real relationship,
disconnect
the virtual ones

Love is
unique,
it hurts
when you are
far,
and senses
when you are
near

FaceTime
does not bring
the spontaneity
in your smile,
your
vibrant laughter
is the best
when
you and I
are together

It looks like
something is
missing,
some sweet

and
some humorous
talk
that was
our identity
and
also our connection,
WhatsApp and
Facebook
have controlled
them

I left
the connected world
today,
to find myself,

You have to meet yourself
You have to find yourself

13. सीख

वो आँखें
कह गयी,
और
इस दिल
ने
सुन भी
लिया

बे मतलब
ही
अब तक
करते रहे,
जुबान
और
कानों
का
इस्तेमाल

13. Learning

Your eyes
speak
and
my heart
listens

I wonder
why have
we
used
words
for
so long

14. हर इक तस्वीर बोलती है

समय थम सा गया है,
तस्वीरों के पलटते पन्नों में
सारी ज़िन्दगी जैसे सामने
आकर रूक सी गयी हो

याद है
ये बर्फीले पहाड़,
हम पहली बार घर से
इतनी दूर आए थे
और तुम बस वहीं पर,
इक नया घर बनाना चाहती थी

उस समुन्दर की लहर में
हाथ थामें धीमे-धीमे
किस कदर खींच रही थी तुम,
और फिर भींगी रेतों मे सीप ढूँढना

हवाओं को भी
तुम्हारी गेसूओं से
इतनी मोहब्बत है,
देखो इनका खेलना

वो शाम अब भी याद है,
देखो इन खूबसूरत
आँखों की चमक
तेज, बेबाक़
जैसे हर पल कुछ करने को आतुर

हर इक तस्वीर की
अपनी कहानी है,
बोलती हैं सब की सब
बोलती हैं सब की सब

14. *Every Picture tells a story*

Time
pauses
while flipping
through
the picture album,
and
the memories come
alive

Do you remember
this mountain
full of snow,
it was the
first time
we had gone
so far
away from home
and
you wanted to
be there
forever

Walking
on that
beach
you were
pulling me

all along
while holding
my hands,
and
then
your sudden stops
to
pick up
those
seashells
from the wet sand

Look at
this picture,
the winds
always loved
your
long hair
and
liked
teasing it

I still
remember
that evening,
the sparkle
in those eyes,
sharp
and
restless

always trying
to
surprise me

Every picture tells a story,
All of them speak

15. कोई बुला तो रहा है

कहीं से आवाज़,
किसी की धड़कन,
किन्हीं की दुआ,
कोई बुला तो रहा है

आज फिर वही आवाज़
कुछ कह गयी हमसे,
अब गूँज लगने लगी,
कोई बुला तो रहा है

दिल की चाहत को
सारी वो धड़कनें अब
महसूस होने लगी हैं,
कोई बुला तो रहा है

चारों तरफ़ दुआएँ
सुनायी देने लगीं,
खुदा का वास्ता,
कोई बुला तो रहा है

15. Someone is calling

Voices all around,
so are
heartbeats
and
prayers,
Someone is calling

The same
voice
talked to me
again
today,
it's
echoing now,
Someone is calling

When the heart is
full of love
it can sense
every beat,
Someone is calling

When you hear
prayers
from every direction,
certainly
Someone is calling

16. मिन्नत

ऐ खुदा
तुझे तो
सब
पता है,
फिर
क्यों नहीं
पूरी
कर देता
है
मुरादें

क्यों
इंतज़ार
करता है
कि हम
मिन्नतें
करें

शायद
माँगने से
लगन
पक्की हो

सुनना
चाहता है,
या
फिर

बार–बार
हमें ही
देता है
मौका

कहते
रहने की,
सुनने की,
कुछ
कर
दिखाने की

16. Wish

O Lord,
You know it all
then why
don't You
fulfill
our ambitions

Why do You
wait
for us
to pray

Perhaps
by asking
You,
we work
more and more
to achieve

Do You
want
to hear more,
or
by doing so
You give us
more
opportunities

to
fulfill
our ambitions
ourselves

17. पचास

पचास साल
सुनने में
ज़्यादा,
सही में
बहुत
कम
होते हैं

कब निकल गये
इतने सारे साल

बच्चे
पहले
इजाज़त
ले कर
बड़ी तहज़ीब से
कुछ भी
किया करते थे,
जब हम
उनके लिये
सुपर-मैन
होते थे

अब,
बता भी दें
तो समझो
इनायत है,

और
अगर कभी
पूछ लिया,
तो
आपको
क्या पता है

अब कोई नहीं पूछता
मेरे लिये क्या लाये हो,
एयरपोर्ट पर
लास्ट मिनट
दुकानों के चक्कर
से छुटकारा,
या
और
एक कप
स्टारबक्स
का मौका

पहले
देर रात को,
फ़्लाइट लेट
होने पर भी
मैडम
साथ खाने का
इंतज़ार करती थी,
अब
खुद गरम करो
और खा भी लो
हाँ,

वो चार पैरों वाला
ज़रूर वेट करता है,
अपने
ट्रीट के लिये
ही सही

माँ सही कहती थी,
जब पचास के हो जाओगे
खुद ही समझ जाओगे

अब बातें
थोड़ी-थोड़ी
समझ में
आती हैं,
पहले
शायद
सिर्फ़
सुनायी
देती थी

माँ सही कहती थी,
हर बार
पूछने या बताने
में वो मज़ा
नहीं,
जो बच्चों के
खुद
कर दिखाने
और सीखने
में है

अब पचास का हूँ,
आँखों को
दिखता तो
पहले
भी था,
अब
दिल से
देखना
सीख
रहा हूँ

तकरार
में तो तुम
पहले भी
जीतती थी,
पर
तुमसे
हारने का
मज़ा
तो अब
निखर कर
आया है

तुम्हारी
खूबसूरती के
तो
हम पहले से ही
दीवाने हैं

अब बाल
लम्बे हो
या छोटे,
खुल के हँसो
या धीरे से,
गुस्सा करो
या मुस्कुराओ,
बातें करो
या चुप रहो

मेरी धड़कन तो
कब की खो चुकी,
अब हर साँस
पे नाम
तुम्हारा है

हर साँस
पे नाम
तुम्हारा है

17. *Fifty*

Fifty years,
although
it appears to be
a lot,
is
actually
quite less

Where did
these
years
go

Earlier
kids would
seek permission
before doing
anything,
when we were
superheroes
to them

Now,
if they even
tell us
we should be
thankful

and
if ever we ask,
then
'what do you know'

Now
no one asks
what did
you bring for me,
no last minute
rush
at the airport shop,
and
perhaps
some
extra time to
grab
that cup of Starbucks

Earlier,
even if
the flight was late
you would wait
at dinner for me,
now
I heat up and eat
by
myself

Though
my pet
does wait,
perhaps
just
to get his treat

My mother was right,
she always said
when you get to fifty,
you would
understand

Earlier
I used to
listen,
now
I
get the
meaning

My mother was right,
there is no fun
in asking or
telling
every time,
kids
learn best
when they
feel

their own
experiences

Now I am fifty,
I used to
see clearly
earlier
as well,
I am
now learning
to see
from
my heart

Sweetheart,
you would
anyway
win
all the
arguments,
though
the joy of losing
to you
is now
getting clearer

I have always
loved you
the way
you are,

whether
with
short hair
or long,
whether
you
laugh out loud
or
give
a gentle smile,
whether
you are angry
or not,
whether
you talk
or
are quiet

My heartbeat
has always been for
you,
now
every breath too is yours,
every breath too is yours

18. आवाज़

कितनी बार
ऐसा लगा,
जैसे
शायद
कुछ कम
सुना

अपनी धुन में
बोलना ज्यादा,
और
सुनना कम
ही
होता है

फिर
तन्हायी में
हर बार
ढूँढतें हैं
वो
आवाज़

जो दिल की
धड़कन है,
कानों को
महसूस
नहीं होती

18. Sound

Many times
it seems like
that you hear
less

When you are
on a mission,
you speak more
and
listen less

Then in
solitude,
you search for
that
sound

That only
the heart can
hear,
ears don't
feel it

19. धड़कन हो मेरे जीवन की

वो उस समय भी
अपना ही लगा,
कुछ बात थी उसमें
इतने सालों के बाद
आज भी जब वो
दिन याद आता है
सारा आलम
झूम सा जाता है

कभी फुरसत से बैठेंगे
तो दिल से पूछ लेंगे हम,
ये धड़कन कैसे जुटती है
मोहब्बत कैसे होती है

उनकी बातों में अक्सर ही
मैंने खुद को ही पाया है,
चाहे कहीं भी रहूँ सनम
मेरे साथ तेरा ही साया है

हवा तू धीरे-धीरे चल
लेने दे खुशबू साँसों में,
ये दो क़दमों की बात नहीं
जन्मों का साथ हमारा है

एक दिन वो था हम कोने से
छुप-छुप कर देखा करते थे,
सपनों में आना जाना था
पलकों पर तब से रखा है

अब कहना क्या
और सुनना क्या,
बातें शुरू हम करतें है
और ख़त्म तुम्हीं पर होती है

मोहब्बत हमने भी की है
मोहब्बत में तो तुम भी हो,
फ़िज़ा मे रंग आ जाता है
जो मुस्कुराओ तुम सनम

बड़ी मिन्नत की है हमने
खुदा से माँगा है तुमको,
दिल ही रहना हरदम तुम
धड़कन हो मेरे जीवन की,
धड़कन हो मेरे जीवन की

19. *You are the heartbeat of my life*

Even then
he appeared to be my own,
there was something
in him,
after so many years,
when I remember
that day
the whole world
looked blissful

When I do get
some time to think,
I will ask
my heart,
how do heartbeats meet,
how do you fall in love

I often find
myself
in his talks,
his shadow
is always with me
whether I am
close or far

Oh wind,

you should move
slowly,
let me inhale
the fragrance,
it's not about
a few steps
this relationship
is
of several lives

There was a day
when I
would look at you
from the hidden corners,
you would appear
in my dreams
I have had you
with me
ever since

Now
what's there to say
and what's there to listen to,
whenever I begin
to talk
it always ends with you

We are both
in love
and

the whole world
looks so beautiful
with
your
simple smile

I have
prayed
for so long
and
have asked the Lord,
you should always stay in my heart

You are the heartbeat of my life,
You are the heartbeat of my life

20. ऐसा क्यूँ होता है

कुछ बूँद आँखों से
यूँ टपक ही जाते हैं,
कौन इनको याद आए
किनको ढूँढतें हैं ये

वो दर्द अक्सर ही
पूछता है हमसे,
क्यों रखा है हमें
इतना सम्भाल कर

कुछ बातें भूल कर भी
जाने भूलती नहीं,
बस यूँ ही बोल जाती हैं
हल्की तन्हायी में

कुछ कह गयी थी तुम
सितम है बार-बार,
अक्सर ही याद आती है
बातें सारी तुम्हारी

बाँहें पकड़ तो लेतीं हैं
दिल सम्भलता फिर भी नहीं,
खो गये हैं सनम हम
तेरे चौखट पे आ कर भी

कितने दिनों के बाद
वो हवा थी चली आज,

पास ले कर तो आयी
फिर उड़ा भी गयी खुशबू

कभी ऐसा भी होता है,
पर
ऐसा क्यूँ होता है,
ऐसा क्यूँ होता है

20. Why does it happen

Some drops fall
from the eyes,
who do they remember
who do they look for

That pain
always asks me,
why have you kept me
with so much care

Sometimes you never forget
those words,
they speak themselves
when you are lonely

You said something,
I wish you had not,
I remember
all that you had said

The hands hold themselves,
The heart does not,
I am lost
at your doorstep

After so many days
that wind was soothing,

it did bring you closer
and
then again took you away

Sometimes
it feels like this,
but
why does it happen,
why does it happen

21. चलो बूढ़े हो चलें

बिन बोले ही बातें सारी
खुद समझ में आ जायें,
धड़कन दिल की अपनी ही
सारी राग सुनाये

साँसों का जुड़ना
अद्भुत है,
दिल तो हैं
कब के एक हुए

इज़हार मेरा, इनकार तुम्हारा
इन सब का
अब दोनों पर,
कुछ भी असर नहीं पड़ता

न मैं कुछ चाहूँ
न तुम कुछ माँगो,
ओह,
अनहोनी सा लगता है

दौड़-भाग कि ज़िन्दगी
कब किसको अच्छी लगती है,
दुनिया भले ही देख लिया
दामन में सारा जीवन है

अब हाथ पकड़ कर हम
चलो बूढ़े हो चलें,

जो कुछ कभी कहा नहीं
वो भी अब सुन सकें

चलो बूढ़े हो चलें,
चलो बूढ़े हो चलें

21. *Let's get old*

Without
even talking
we
understand
what's said,
our heartbeats
themselves
play
the whole
symphony

Our hearts
have been
one
for
such a while,
it's magical
for our breaths
to
be in concert

Yes
or no
it doesn't
matter
any longer,

I don't
desire
and
you don't
ask
for anything,
Oh,
those appear
quite unreal

No one
wants
to
run around
constantly,
even if
one has
seen
the whole world,
the real meaning
of life
is to be
with
each other

Let's
hold hands
and
let's
get old,

let's hear
what has
never
been said before

Let's get old,
Let's get old

22. निहारना

तमाम उम्र
मैं
तुझे
निहारता रहा

और,
हर वक़्त
तुम
मुझे
ढूँढती रही

22. Search

My
entire life
I have been
looking
at you

And,
the
entire time
you kept
searching
for
me

23. महसूस

मुहब्बत
महसूस
की जाती है

कोई ज़रूरी तो नहीं
कि हर वक़्त
लबों पर,
दिल कि बात
आ ही जाये

23. *Feel*

You
must feel
the love

Our lips
can't
always
say,
what
the heart
wants

24. जवाब

वो नग़में
जो कल
तक
कुछ और
लगते थे,
आज
अचानक
हमें इशारा
कर
रहे हैं

अख़बार के
पन्नों से
ख़बरें भी,
जैसे
कुछ
कह रहीं हों
मुझसे

बाज़ार का
कोलाहल
बातें
करते लोग,
पहले,
सिर्फ़ हल्ला
लगता था,
इनसे भी

अब मैं
कुछ
सीख रहा हूँ

टीवी पर
आ रही
फिल्म के
किरदारों की
बातों में,
जैसे
मैं
अपनी ही
कहानी
सुन रहा हूँ

जिन सवालों
के जवाब
हम
ढूँढते
रहते हैं,
वो
शायद,
हर वक़्त
हमारे
आस-पास
ही
होते हैं

24. Answer

Those songs
till
yesterday
were
simply songs,
now
they have
started
telling me
something

News from
the papers
have also
started
talking to
me

People's chatter,
noises
in the
market,
were earlier
just sounds,
now
I have started
learning

something
from them

Dialogues
from the movie
are telling
my own
stories

Answers
to the
questions
that we
seek,
are
perhaps,
always
around us

25. बातें

ना वो
सवाल था,
ना उसका
जवाब है

चलो
कुछ
ऐसी बातें,
कभी कहें
और
सुने भी

25. *Talk*

It
is not
a question,
and
there is
no answer

Sometimes,
let's
simply
talk

26. माँ

हर सप्ताह
ट्रन्क-काल पर
बातें होती
और
हर बार,
अपना
ख़्याल रखना
ठीक से
खाना तो खाते हो
ज़्यादा रात तक
जग कर
पढ़ते नहीं रहना
सेहत का ध्यान रखना
इम्तहान तो
अच्छा ही होगा

छुट्टियों में
घर आया,
इस बार
दरवाज़े पर
नहीं दिखी
माँ,
दो महीनों से
बिस्तर पर ही हैं

दो महीने पहले
बाथरूम में फिसलना

और पैरों की हड्डी,
उफ़

और,
इतने दिनों तक
हर सप्ताह
हर बार
उसी तरह से
फोन पर
मुझसे बातें,

अपना
ख़्याल ज़रूर रखना
अपना
ख़्याल ज़रूर रखना

26. Mother

I would talk
to
my mother
every week,
on
long distance calls
and
everytime
she would say,
take care of
yourself,
eat properly,
don't study too late,
your exams
will be
just fine

I came home
for holidays,
and
didn't see
her
at the
door

She had slipped

in the bathroom
and
fractured
her leg,
she
has been
bedridden
for
two months

And,
still
every week
on the
phone
she would say,
take care of yourself,
take care of yourself

27. दुआ

कभी जो
बुझ गयी
थी रौशनी
और
रास्ते भी
सारे बंद
थे

गिर कर
लगा
जैसे कि
उठना तो
अब
मुमकिन नहीं

अगर हूँ
यहाँ
तो
मान ले

तेरी
दुआ
में
रब
तो है

27. *Prayer*

When
there was
total darkness
and
all roads
were
closed

When
standing up
after
falling down
seemed
impossible
for a while

If
I am
still here
then
you
must know
your
prayers have
power

28. पहेली

तुम
अपनों को
ढूँढते रहे,
हम
अपने से
दूर
हो गये

कभी
पूछते थे
आपसे,
अब
समझते हैं
खुद को

जो कहा
वो
सुन लिया,
जो
ना कहा
कुछ और है

जो
दिख गया
वो सामने,
और
ना दिखे

वो भी
तो है

वो जो
ना
भी था
तो सच,
और
जो
सच है,
वो तो
है ही

एक पहेली ही है जीवन,
एक पहेली ही है जीवन

28. Riddle

You
kept looking
for
your own,
and
I
moved away
from
myself

Earlier
I used
to ask
you,
now
I
try to
understand
myself

I heard
what
you said,
and
also
what
you didn't

What
you see
is
in front
of you,
what you
don't
also
exists

What was
not there
was true,
and
the truth
is always
true

Isn't life
a riddle

29. हक़ीक़त

अर्ज़ियाँ
दे कर
मुहब्बत
तो
की नहीं
हमने

पूछा भी नहीं
किसी से
कि
रहती कहाँ
हो तुम

जहाँ तेरी
ख़ुशबू मिली
उन रास्तों
पर
चल पड़े

वो दुप्पटा
जो है
उड़ रहा,
वो हँसी
जो है
खिल रही,
बेक़ाबू धड़कन
है अपनी

लगता है
तुम हो
यहीं कहीं

कल जो
देखा नहीं
तुझे,
लगता है
बरसों बीत
गये,
ये प्यार
जो
पागलपन
सा है
वो मीठी
याद
तुम्हारी है

मुहब्बत ही हक़ीक़त है,
मुहब्बत ही हक़ीक़त है

29. Reality

Didn't fill
an application
to fall in love

Didn't ask anyone
where you live

I just followed
the path
that had
your lingering fragrance

The flying scarf,
the bubbling smile,
raises my heartbeat
when you are nearby

It feels like ages
since I saw you yesterday,
your sweet memories
are making me
fall in love again

Love is reality

30. ऐनिवरसरी

मोहब्बत में
दिन
और
साल
नहीं गिने

हर पल में
हो जादू,
यही आरजू भी
और
दुआ भी की

30. *Anniversary*

In love
don't
count
days
and
years

Letting
every moment
be magical,
is
the desire
and
also
the prayer

31. छोटी-छोटी यादें

क्या लिखूँ
और
क्या कहूँ,
बड़ी बातें
बड़ी यादें
तो
जैसे हर-दम
होती है,
चलो
कुछ और कहें
कुछ और सुनें,
छोटी-छोटी
बातें

वो
पहली मुलाक़ात,
कुर्सी छोड़
उस
क़ालीन पर
बैठना,
शायद
उससे
कुछ
ज़्यादा ही
लगाव था
जो

इस क़दर
अपने
रंग भरे
ख़ूबसूरत नाख़ून
से
उसे तराशना,
जब तक
हमारी बातें
ख़त्म हुई
वो भी
खिल गया था

हल्की सी चोट
कुछ टाँके,
दर्द
मुझे था
महसूस
तुम कर रही थी,
सुबह
जब नींद खुली
तुम्हारा
एक टक
से देखना,
रात
ऐसे ही
गुज़ार दी थी
तुमने

इतने दिन
हो गये

ट्रैवल
करते हुए,
अब भी
वो धड़कन
जो
महसूस होती है
घर
आने वाले
प्लेन में
बैठने
के पहले,
वो
कुछ और
ही होती है

वो डाक्टर
भी
जैसे हैरान,
कितनी बार
उसने पूछा
खुद
चल कर
कैसे
आ गयी,
अभी
तो चार दिन
भी
नहीं गुज़रे
इतनी बड़ी
सर्जरी हुए,

उसने तो
सिर्फ़
नसें और
खून देखी थी,
हिम्मत और
विश्वास
तो
मुझे पता है

बस,
कुछ
छोटी-छोटी
यादें ही
बन जाती हैं
ज़िन्दगी,

छोटी-छोटी
यादें ही
बन जाती हैं
ज़िन्दगी

31. Small memories

What should
I write
and tell,
big stories
big memories
are always
there,
let's talk about
some
small
beautiful memories

That first meeting,
after
some time
of talking
you
moved away
from the chair
to sit
and
relax
on the carpet,
and
by the time
we finished
our talk

the carpet had
all the color
from your
toenails

A few
stitches
from that
cut,
I was in pain
and
you were feeling it,
I saw it in your eyes
when I woke up,
you were up
all night

I have been
traveling
for such
a long time,
even now
the
flight back home
always has
a different
heartbeat

The doctor

was surprised
that you had gone
there
all by
yourself
just four days
after the surgery,
He had only
seen
your veins and blood,
I have seen
your courage
and faith

Life is full of small memories,
They become life

32. सेल्फ़ी

वो
निश्चल हँसी
वो
हल्की मुस्कुराहट,
फिर कहीं
अल्लहड़ सी
मस्ती भरी,
ठहाकों वाली गूँज

कुछ अनोखा
अंदाज़
है तुम्हारा

सम्भाल कर
रखना इन्हें

खुद से
खुद की
खींची
तस्वीरों
ने,
अभी
वो जादू,
वो नज़ाकत
नहीं सीखा

जब भी मिलो
अपनी वाली ही
मुस्कान रखना,
सेल्फ़ी वाली नहीं

32. *Selfie*

Your
simple laugh
your
gentle smile,
and
then again
your
roaring laughter

Your style
is
simply unique,
always
be yourself

Pictures
that
you take
yourself,
could never
capture
your charm,
your elegance

When
we meet,
smile

your smile,
and
not
the ones
you have
in
selfies

33. आराम

नींद
को भी
आराम
अब
मुमकिन
नहीं

हर बार
सपनों में
तुम
आ ही
जाती हो

33. *Rest*

Even
sleep
doesn't
go
to rest

You
always
appear
in
my dream

34. अस्पताल

कितनी बार
पूछा उसने

मैं कहाँ हूँ,
क्यों यहाँ हूँ,
कब से हूँ

तुम कौन हो,
क्यों मेरे पास
बैठे हो,
वो कौन है,
वो क्या
कर रही है

पिछले
चार दिनों से
देख रहा हूँ

हर दिन
जब भी
उसे
होश आया,
फिर से
वही सारी
बातें

और
हर बार
बेटे और माँ ने,
हाथ थाम कर
फिर से
उसी तरह से
मुस्कुरा कर
वही बातें
फिर से
दोहरायीं

34. Hospital

How many times
he asked

Where am I,
why am I here,
for how long

Who are you,
why are you
sitting with me,
who is she,
what is she doing

This has been going on
for the last four days

Everyday when
he gains
consciousness,
same questions,
and
every day
his son and wife
answer
with the same smile
to bring life back

35. समय

लोग
आते रहे,
सब की
बातें भी
सुनी,
और
मिलना भी
हो गया

काफी
पुरानी बातें
हो
रहीं हैं,
कुछ तो
अब
मुझे
याद भी
नहीं

उन
गुलदस्तों
के
फूलों की
खुशबू
इतनी
प्यारी है,
लगा जैसे

बस
पकड़े ही
रहूँ

आज सारे
इतनी
प्रशंसा
क्यों
कर रहें हैं,
चलो
अब
कुछ आगे
के लिये
तो
छोड़ दो

और
हाँ,
कुछ हँस
भी लो
अब
बातें
कुछ ज़्यादा
गंभीर
होने
लगीं हैं

इतनी भीड़
में भी
इस क़दर

शांति
और
सुकून
पहले
तो कभी
नहीं लगा

समय
थम
ही गया है,
अब
नहीं हूँ
मैं

35. *Time*

People kept coming,
I met everyone
and
heard them too

Lots of old stories
being shared,
some
even I
don't remember

Those bouquets
are so nice,
I want to
hold them forever

Everyone is speaking
graciously
about me,
it's so
humbling,
let's leave some
speeches
for
the next time too

And

laugh,
don't be
that serious

So many people
around here,
yet
I find
myself calm
and
composed,
this has never happened
before

Time has just stopped,
I am not here

36. शतरंज

चलो
आज
मोहरा
बन कर देखें

पता
तो चले,
एक को बचाने
हम
इतने सारे,
क्यों
मरते हैं

36. Chess

Let's
play as
pawns
today

Let's find
out,
why
so many of
us
sacrifice
ourselves,
to
advance a few

37. उड़ जाओ

सिले होंठों
से
कहना है,
गले मिल
के
ही
सुनना है,
नमी आँखों
कि बातें
तो
कभी बोली
नहीं जाती

नयनों ने
रोका
अश्क़ों को,
जुबां तो
फिर
भी
हैं गीली,
जो
दिल की
बातें
होती हैं
वो
खुद ही

बोल
जाती हैं

वो क़दम
जो
आगे
रखा है,
उड़ने को
हैं तैयार
ये,
हिम्मत की
पहचान
तुम्हारे
विश्वास भरे
बाजुओं में
है

पक्के इरादे
पाओ तुम,
सारी दुनिया
पर
छाओ तुम,
दिल की
कशिश को
जोड़ो

उड़ जाओ,
उड़ जाओ,
उड़ जाओ

37. *Go fly*

Nothing spoken,
lips pursed tight,
can only sense
from the hug you gave,
though teary eyes
speak for themselves

No words possible,
the heart
finds a way to speak,
even with
choked emotions

You are about to fly
with
just that one
little step forward,
strength visible
from your strong
determination

Be resolute
in your
conviction,
make yourself
proud,

listen to your
heart

Go fly,
Go fly,
Go fly

38. जीतना तो ज़रूरी है

लहू
जो दिख गये,
रंग उनके
कभी
गहरे नहीं होते

वो खून ही क्या
जो गिर गया

दिलों में
आग हो
तो तप कर भी,
सींचो लहू अपना

उबलते खून में
जादू है
अंगारों पर
चल कर देखो

हौसला बुलंद करना होगा
उम्मीदों को उड़ना होगा,
दिशाओं को आना ही है
मंज़िलों को पाना भी है

जीतना तो ज़रूरी है,
जीतना तो ज़रूरी है

38. *Win we must*

Color of blood
that comes out,
is
not deep
enough

Falling
blood
doesn't
serve
the
purpose

If you need
blood
to
fire up
your
heart,
keep
it inside
and
boiling

It does have
magic,
try it

by walking
a path
full of
difficulties

Keep the aspirations high
dreams must fly,
directions will appear
destinations will be near

Win we must,
Win we must

39. दौड़

कभी
ऐसा भी
होता है,
कि
क़दम
थक से
जाते हैं

चल कर
या
दौड़ कर
नहीं,
मन
के बोझ
मार
जाते हैं

ढूँढो
फिर से
उस उद्देश्य
को,
जुनून
ने
जिसकी
दिशा
दी थी

करो
इरादे
मज़बूत,
मंज़िल
तो
पानी ही
है

और
फिर
शुरू करो,
एक
नयी दौड़

39. Chase

Sometimes
legs get tired,
not from
walking or
running,
but
from the
burden
on the mind

Remind yourself
of
the purpose,
that
had sparked
the sense of
direction

Make
a resolve
to reach
the
destination

And
start
afresh,
a
new chase

Acknowledgements

If there is one person who always reminds me of my poems when I need an energy boost it's my wife, Sushma. She knows all of my writings and poems, even more than I do. This book would not be possible without her loving and continuous asking, 'When are you completing it?'

After the launch of the first book, several book reading sessions across the US and India and a new job, clearly writing the second book of poems was not on my priority list. Without Sushma's continuous prodding and gentle reminders I don't think I could have made this happen.

Most of my writing happens on long flights, coast to coast in the US and international flights around the world. Sometimes I write a few paragraphs and ask her about the flow and the theme in real time (provided the Wi-Fi is working on the flight!). She either gives me a thumbs up or sends a cryptic note, hinting to stick to the theme. Occasionally, I get a simple, 'Hmmm.'

Big hug and thanks to Shikha Singh and Khyati Patel for reading the draft while they both had their respective semester exams. I guess they found reading poems more enlightening! Big love to Soumya Srivatsa for his constant follow through on both books, getting the needed draft copy and input to meet the deadline for submission.

Sincere thanks to my parents, Asha Singh and Dr. Harendra Kishore Singh, and my in-laws, Uma Rani Rai and Dr. Rama Kant Rai, for taking the time to review the poems in their early stages and for providing key input.

My heartfelt gratitude to Harsh Goenka for writing the foreword for this book. It is truly an honor and privilege to work with him.

Thank you so much Chau Heather Crawford, Libbi Thevenet and Lisa Lujan for your amazing help, insights and input.

Thanks to all of my friends and colleagues who have heard me recite my poems at several events. Thank you for your support and affection.

Special thanks to Kapish Mehra, Managing Director at Rupa Publications, for always being available with his very insightful inputs. Thanks to Elina Majumdar, Managing Editor and Rudra Narayan Sharma, Commissioning Editor at Rupa Publications for providing much-needed editorial help. This book is finally published, thanks to their phenomenal support.

Thanks to all of my friends who helped me with my first book, *Your Shadow Wants to Walk Alone*. Clearly this book, *Old Old Seeds of a New Tree*, would not be possible without the success of the first one.

I want to thank all of my readers who write to me about how they connect with the poems. Your affection and support are the key reasons for getting my second book, *Old*

Old Seeds of a New Tree. Thank you very much for your support and confidence. I do hope you like these poems.
Love to you all.

Cause, Commit and Support

I commit that net proceeds from this book will be donated to the cause of skill development and vocational training programs through our foundation, *Har Asha Foundation*.

By 2025, only an estimated five percent of the quarter-billion people entering the workforce in India will have formal vocational training. The gap between the supply and demand of skilled workers is especially pronounced for youths. Ninety percent of India's youth works in the informal sector, learning on the job without any structured or formal training. The lack of market-relevant skills often leads them to settle for a life of low-paying jobs. We believe that as urbanization in India increases and cities of millions become the norm, this gap will increase even more.

Har Asha Foundation supports the efforts in the area of skills development and vocational training. We believe structured and market-relevant training programs will enable youths to gain the competencies required to bridge the gap between the supply and demand of skilled workers. For every skill taught, each youth gains training. For every apprentice placed, each youth gains experience. For every graduate of such programs, each path to a skilled job is created. We know that each enabled person can make a positive difference to the local ecosystem. We know that enabling more youths will create even more positive ripples throughout larger ecosystems.

Har Asha Foundation believes in enabling people and enabling the world.

At *Har Asha Foundation*, we believe that every hope needs to be nurtured, every hope needs a chance and every hope needs an opportunity to become real.

Thank you for your kind and generous support to this cause. Fore more information, please visit:

www.harashafoundation.org